Our Song

The Story of "O Canada"

Peter Kuitenbrouwer

Ashley Spires

Scholastic Canada Ltd.
Toronto New York London Auckland Sydney
Mexico City New Delhi Hong Kong Buenos Aires

To Mimi, Tallulah and Frits — Yours, Peter
For Grandma Joan — Ashley Spires

The art for this book was made with illustration and digital collage.

Scholastic Canada Ltd.
604 King Street West, Toronto, Ontario M5V 1E1, Canada

Scholastic Inc.
557 Broadway, New York, NY 10012, USA

Scholastic Australia Pty Limited
PO Box 579, Gosford, NSW 2250, Australia

Scholastic New Zealand Limited
Private Bag 94407, Botany, Manukau 2163, New Zealand

Scholastic Children's Books
Euston House, 24 Eversholt Street, London NW1 1DB, UK

www.scholastic.ca

Library and Archives Canada Cataloguing in Publication

Kuitenbrouwer, Peter, 1962-, author
Our song : the story of O Canada / Peter Kuitenbrouwer ; illustrated by
Ashley Spires.
Includes the text of O Canada, in English and French.
ISBN 978-1-4431-0236-0 (paperback)
1. Lavallée, Calixa, 1842-1891. O Canada--Juvenile literature. 2. National
songs--Canada--History and criticism--Juvenile literature. I. Spires, Ashley,
1978-, illustrator II. Title.
ML3563.K965 2017   j782.42'15990971   C2016-907990-2

Map illustrations: Malcolm Cullen
"O Canada" sheet music arrangement by Fabrizio Ferrari, courtesy of virtualsheetmusic.com
Photograph of Robert Stanley Weir courtesy of Matthew Farfan Collection

6 5 4 3 2   Printed in Canada 119   17 18 19 20 21

FSC
www.fsc.org
MIX
Paper from
responsible sources
FSC® C103113

O Canada! Our home and native land!
True patriot love thou dost in us command.
We see thee rising fair, dear land,
The True North, strong and free;
And stand on guard, O Canada,
We stand on guard for thee.

The original first verse of Robert Stanley Weir's poem
O Canada, written in 1908.

O Canada!

Canada's Song

O Canada: We stand and sing it at hockey, baseball, and football games, and at the start of every school day. When our athletes triumph at the Olympics, arenas fill with the melody. At Remembrance Day ceremonies, we pay tribute with this song. But where does it come from?

O Canada started small, just like the nation. In the time of gas lamps and horse-drawn carriages, partygoers sang the first version of the anthem, in French, in Québec City. Then the song spread east and west, picking up English words as it travelled. Before there was radio or TV, *O Canada* became our first pop hit, sung in dozens of versions everywhere, from Royal visits to the battlefields of Europe.

Finally in 1980, 100 years after the song's birth, *O Canada* became the official anthem of our country. This is the story of that great journey, from a tune written by a waterfall to the anthem we sing today across the land.

O Ca - na - da!   Our home and na - tive land,
O Ca - na - da!   ter - re de nos aï - eux,

True pa - triot love   in all thy sons com - mand.
Ton front est ceint   de fleu - rons glo - ri - eux !

TIMELINE: 1880-1900

1875 — The Supreme Court of Canada is established.

1880 — Calixa Lavallée composes the music of *O Canada*, to accompany the poem by Adolphe-Basile Routhier.

1880 — Emily Stowe, long considered Canada's first female doctor, is finally granted a license to practice.

1885 — Canada's cross-country railway is completed! The last spike is set in Eagle Pass, B.C.

1885 — Louis Riel leads the North West Rebellion. The Métis are defeated at Batoche and Riel is executed.

1891 — Canadian Louis Cyr, The Strongest Man in the World, keeps four horses in check with the sheer force of his arms.

1896 — Edison's projected moving picture machine, the Vitascope, shows the first movie to be seen in Canada.

1897 — The Klondike gold rush begins.

1898 — The Yukon becomes a district separate from the Northwest Territories.

1899 — The Boer War begins in South Africa; Canada sends its troops to fight overseas for the first time.

Born in a waterfall

Calixa Lavallée (1842-1891)
National Archives of Canada

Picture St. Hyacinthe, Québec, a small town southeast of Montréal, on a sunny morning in April, 1880. The warm sun has melted the snow, and sent it rushing into creeks. The ice has broken and the water rages down the mighty Yamaska River.

By the Yamaska falls, a tired man sits down to rest. His name is Calixa Lavallée. After many years of travel, he is back in St. Hyacinthe where he grew up. Here are the streets where Calixa, son of a black-smith, kicked around a ball. Here is the cathedral where, at age nine, Calixa played for pilgrims after the organist took sick.

Calixa wanted to see the world. On a visit to Montréal when he was fifteen, Calixa saw a travelling music show so magical he followed the minstrels far away to New Orleans. From there, the young musician voyaged as a violinist to Mexico and Brazil, returned to the United States, and signed up for the Union army to fight in the bloody American Civil War.

Such adventures! He lived in New York, Paris and London, gaining fame for the operas he composed along the way. Sailing home in 1880, he found his young country buzzing with plans for a June celebration of the French in North America. Aware of Lavallée's international fame as a talented composer, the party planners asked him for some music to mark the occasion. The story goes that while home in St. Hyacinthe to give a concert, there, resting by the Yamaska waterfall, Calixa Lavallée heard in the pounding water the rousing tune: *O Canada.*

The words of the song came from another son of Québec, Adolphe-Basile Routhier. Born in 1839, Routhier grew up northwest of Montréal, in the small town of St. Placide, in a stone house his father built on the shores of the lac des Deux Montagnes.

As a boy, Routhier listened to the work songs of loggers who rode rafts down the lake in spring and the music of Iroquois trappers who paddled up the lake in fall. These songs inspired him for many years to come. Although he grew up to study law, and eventually became Chief Justice of Québec, Routhier was as well known for the many poems and books he wrote under the name Jean Piquefort. In 1880, as an organizer of the Québec City festivities, he was asked to write the French words of *O Canada*. His lyrics have never since been altered:

O Canada! Terre de nos aïeux,
Ton front est ceint de fleurons glorieux!
Car ton bras sait porter l'épée,
Il sait porter la croix!
Ton histoire est une épopée
Des plus brillants exploits.
Et ta valeur, de foi trempée,
Protégera nos foyers et nos droits.
Protégera nos foyers et nos droits.

With glow - ing hearts we see thee rise, The true north strong and free!
Car ton bras sait por - ter l'é - pé - e, Il sait por - ter la croix.

TIMELINE: 1900-1920

1901 — The first Transatlantic radio message is received in St. John's, Newfoundland.

1904 — Canada officially receives its first Olympic gold medal thanks to Etienne Desmarteau in the hammer throw event.

1905 — Alberta and Saskatchewan become Canadian provinces.

1907 — At Toronto's Massey Hall, an English version of *O Canada* is heard for the very first time.

1912 — The Titanic sinks off the coast of Newfoundland. Recovered bodies are buried in a Halifax cemetery.

1914 — The Canadian Pacific ocean liner, the Empress of Ireland, sinks in the St. Lawrence River.

1914 — Canadian soldiers sent off to fight in the First World War under the leadership of PM Robert Borden.

1916 — Women in Manitoba become the first females in Canada to vote.

1917 — The National Hockey League (NHL) is officially formed.

1917 — The Mont-Blanc explodes in the Halifax Harbour, instantly killing 1500.

O Canada: It's a hit!

ON JUNE 24, 1880, St. Jean-Baptiste Day, 500 guests sat down at six immense tables in Québec City's Pavillon des Patineurs, a skating rink. They had gathered to celebrate French culture in Canada, a country that their families had proudly called home for over 200 years. After a sumptuous meal of roasted meats and mouth-watering pies, the band started up. "Electrified by an unstoppable impulse," reported those who were there, the crowd stood and sang, for the first time, *O Canada*, the song born in a waterfall.

In 1891, Calixa Lavallée died, penniless and forgotten, in Boston. Like many great artists, he did not become famous while he was alive. His poor health plagued him, and a streak of bad luck reduced his income to zero. His song, though, was steadily becoming a hit.

O Canada swept Québec first. Judge Routhier wrote in a 1907 letter that it had been sung "hundreds and hundreds of times, in the music halls, in the theatres, in the churches, in all the festivities."

In the fall of 1901, the Duke and Duchess of York, later King George V and Queen Mary, toured Canada. In Québec City, 3,000 school children performed *O Canada* for them in French.

In Toronto, on October 12, 1901, the Duke, mounted on a white horse, inspected Canadian troops. The infantry played the troops' march: *O Canada*. It was one of the first times the public outside Québec heard the song.

The conductor of Toronto's famed Mendelssohn choir heard *O Canada* that day and asked, "What is that wonderful thing?" Dr. Thomas Bedford Richardson, who had learned the music of *O Canada* while serving in the army at Niagara Camp, wrote a translation of the French words:

> O Canada! Our fathers' land of old
> Thy brow is crown'd with leaves of red and gold.
> Beneath the shade of the Holy Cross
> Thy children own their birth
> No stains thy glorious annals gloss
> Since valour shield thy hearth.
> Almighty God! On thee we call
> Defend our rights, forfend this nation's thrall,
> Defend our rights, forfend this nation's thrall.

Judge Routhier was favorably impressed by the translation, and in 1907 the Mendelssohn Choir gave the first English choral performance of *O Canada* at Toronto's Massey Hall.

From far and wide, O Ca - na - da!
Ton his - toire est une é - po - pé - e

We stand on guard for thee.
Des plus bril- lants ex - ploits

TIMELINE: 1920-1940

1921
Agnes MacPhail becomes the first woman elected to Parliament in Canada.

1921
Dr. Banting and Charles H. Best discover insulin, a key treatment in controlling diabetes.

1924
The Red Ensign becomes Canada's official flag.

1927
Labrador is awarded to Newfoundland, rather than Québec, by Britain's Privy Council.

1927
Canada officially publishes the Weir version of *O Canada* for the Diamond Jubilee.

1933
Canadian Fay Wray stars as the screaming heroine of Hollywood blockbuster *King Kong*.

1934
The Dionne quintuplets are born in Corbeil, Ontario.

1936
The Canadian Broadcasting Corporation (CBC) is established.

1936
Joseph Shuster, a Canadian expatriate, creates the comic book character *Superman*.

1939
Canada enters World War II under the leadership of PM Mackenzie King.

The Search for English Words

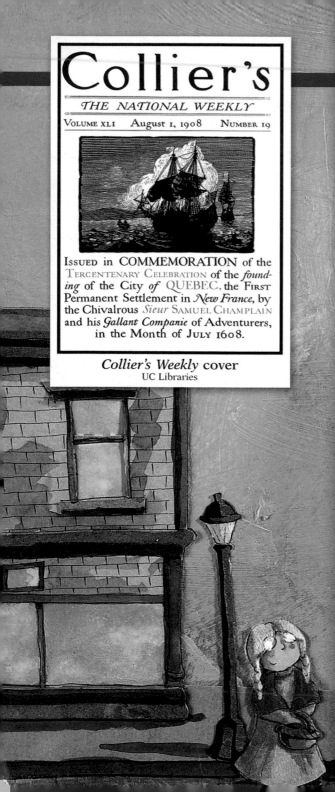

Something in Lavallée's music stirred people across the nation. But Dr. Richardson's translation of the French words did not catch on in English Canada. As such, new and unofficial English lyrics for *O Canada* began springing up as people set to writing their own versions.

Collier's Weekly, then a popular U.S. magazine stuffed with advertising for fine clothes, shaving soap and cars, launched a Canadian edition in 1908. A year later, wanting to tap into the spirit of the young nation, the magazine launched a contest for English words to *O Canada*. *Collier's* wrote that the melody had taken hold of Canadians "with a bulldog grip. It is a common experience to stand on the rear end of a streetcar and hear a boy [...] absent-mindedly whistling it. The people, great and small have the melody. The aim of this competition has been to give them words."

About 350 people flooded *Colliers'* offices with poems. The judges finally awarded the prize to Emma Powell McCulloch, a graduate from the University of Toronto and mother of two, for her version:

> O Canada! in praise of thee we sing;
> From echoing hills our anthems proudly ring.
> With fertile plains and mountains grand
> With lakes and rivers clear,
> Eternal beauty, thou dost stand
> Throughout the changing year.
> Lord God of Hosts! We now implore
> Bless our dear land this day and evermore,
> Bless our dear land this day and evermore.

Hector Charlesworth, a music critic at the *Toronto Mail and Empire*, praised the lyrics as a wonderful poem. It was a song that would be easy to sing and easier to memorize. "Our task is done," he pronounced, "Let the strains of the new *O Canada!* Be heard throughout the land."

Robert Stanley Weir (1856-1926)
Farfan Collection

Despite Mr. Charlesworth's grand prediction, McCulloch's lyrics failed to capture the heart of Canadians. Still, people were hooked on the tune. World War I increased its recognition and spread its fame. At St. Paul's cathedral in London in 1915, those gathered at a memorial service for Canadian soldiers fallen in the battle of Ypres sang: "O Canada! Thy land of noble name." When Canadian soldiers marched on the Belgian city of Mons, on November 11, 1918, the city's ancient church bells pealed the melody of *O Canada*.

In 1925, William Lyon Mackenzie King, then Prime Minister of Canada, wanted to publish the song in English and French to mark the Diamond Jubilee—Canada's 60th Birthday. But still no one could agree on the English words. King's government wrote to patriotic Canadian groups in every province, asking whether they sang *O Canada* and, if so, which version?

Clubs from Truro, Nova Scotia, to Victoria, B.C., flooded him with dozens of lyrics. But most prominent among the replies was a version of *O Canada* written by a Montréal judge, Robert Stanley Weir.

Weir had written his version of *O Canada* in 1908. At the time, the events of the Red River Rebellion divided the opinions of French and English Canada. With the future of his country on his mind, Weir sat down at his piano. Staring out onto Lake Memphremagog from his summer home near the town of Stanstead, Québec, he played Lavallée's melody and composed these words: "O Canada, our home and native land."

Rather than try to translate the French words, as others had done before him, Weir wanted to catch the spirit of the song and nation. That same year, the *New Educational Music Course*, a book commonly used in schools across the country, published his version of *O Canada*. His lyrics spread quickly and by 1925, Prime Minister King realized that Weir's lyrics captured what Canadians had been searching for.

In 1927, Canada officially published Robert Stanley Weir's lyrics for the Diamond Jubilee.

God keep our land   glo - rious and free!

Et ta va - leur,   de foi trem - pée,

God keep our land   glo - rious and free!
Et ta va - leur,   de foi trem - pée,

God keep our land   glo - rious and free!
Et ta va - leur,   de foi trem - pée,

TIMELINE: 1940-1960

1942
Japanese Canadians are forced into internment camps for the length of WWII, though no charges are ever laid.

1944
Canadian troops land in Normandy on D-Day and take part in the liberation of Holland.

1945
Maurice "Rocket" Richard of the Montreal Canadiens scores 50 goals in 50 games.

1947
Canadian citizenship is introduced. Citizenship certificates help to shape a unique and independent Canadian identity.

1949
Newfoundland joins Confederation, becoming Canada's 10th province.

1951
The National Ballet of Canada is founded.

1952
Canada's first television stations begin broadcasting from Toronto and Montreal.

1957
Future Canadian Prime Minister Lester B. Pearson wins a Nobel Peace Prize for his work with the UN.

1960
Canada's First Nations population wins the right to vote in federal elections.

1960
The Canadian Bill of Rights is passed.

A Gift to the Nation

In 1980, THE 100TH BIRTHDAY of *O Canada*, the nation witnessed one of the worst crises in its history. The people of Québec voted on a plan to make their province a separate country. Luckily for Canada, the plan was rejected. About 60% of the voters in Québec chose to keep their province part of the country.

Canada remained united! In Ottawa, the nation's capital, the leaders of the Canadian government wanted to do something special to celebrate. But it was not going to be easy. The Members of Parliament, who represented many different political parties in the House of Commons, were more accustomed to opposing each other than working together.

But for once, they chose to agree. On June 27th, 1980, the Honourable Francis Fox, Canada's Secretary of State, stood up in the House of Commons. Since World War I, he began, everyone, from soldiers to sailors to hockey players, has sung *O Canada*. To celebrate the renewed unity of Canada, Fox suggested the government should "set the example by enshrining one of the most unifying realities of our young collective history, *O Canada*."

Commemorative stamp: *O Canada* music
Copyright Canada Post Corporations, 1980.
Reproduced with Permission

A Gift to the Nation

IN 1980, THE 100TH BIRTHDAY of *O Canada*, the nation witnessed one of the worst crises in its history. The people of Québec voted on a plan to make their province a separate country. Luckily for Canada, the plan was rejected. About 60% of the voters in Québec chose to keep their province part of the country.

Canada remained united! In Ottawa, the nation's capital, the leaders of the Canadian government wanted to do something special to celebrate. But it was not going to be easy. The Members of Parliament, who represented many different political parties in the House of Commons, were more accustomed to opposing each other than working together.

Commemorative stamp: *O Canada* music
Copyright Canada Post Corporations, 1980.
Reproduced with Permission

But for once, they chose to agree. On June 27th, 1980, the Honourable Francis Fox, Canada's Secretary of State, stood up in the House of Commons. Since World War I, he began, everyone, from soldiers to sailors to hockey players, has sung *O Canada*. To celebrate the renewed unity of Canada, Fox suggested the government should "set the example by enshrining one of the most unifying realities of our young collective history, *O Canada*."

TIMELINE: 1940-1960

1942
Japanese Canadians are forced into internment camps for the length of WWII, though no charges are ever laid.

1944
Canadian troops land in Normandy on D-Day and take part in the liberation of Holland.

1945
Maurice "Rocket" Richard of the Montreal Canadiens scores 50 goals in 50 games.

1947
Canadian citizenship is introduced. Citizenship certificates help to shape a unique and independent Canadian identity.

1949
Newfoundland joins Confederation, becoming Canada's 10th province.

1951
The National Ballet of Canada is founded.

1952
Canada's first television stations begin broadcasting from Toronto and Montreal.

1957
Future Canadian Prime Minister Lester B. Pearson wins a Nobel Peace Prize for his work with the UN.

1960
Canada's First Nations population wins the right to vote in federal elections.

1960
The Canadian Bill of Rights is passed.

TIMELINE: 1940-1960

1942
Japanese Canadians are forced into internment camps for the length of WWII, though no charges are ever laid.

1944
Canadian troops land in Normandy on D-Day and take part in the liberation of Holland.

1945
Maurice "Rocket" Richard of the Montreal Canadiens scores 50 goals in 50 games.

1947
Canadian citizenship is introduced. Citizenship certificates help to shape a unique and independent Canadian identity.

1949
Newfoundland joins Confederation, becoming Canada's 10th province.

1951
The National Ballet of Canada is founded.

1952
Canada's first television stations begin broadcasting from Toronto and Montreal.

1957
Future Canadian Prime Minister Lester B. Pearson wins a Nobel Peace Prize for his work with the UN.

1960
Canada's First Nations population wins the right to vote in federal elections.

1960
The Canadian Bill of Rights is passed.

A Gift to the Nation

IN 1980, THE 100TH BIRTHDAY of *O Canada*, the nation witnessed one of the worst crises in its history. The people of Québec voted on a plan to make their province a separate country. Luckily for Canada, the plan was rejected. About 60% of the voters in Québec chose to keep their province part of the country.

Canada remained united! In Ottawa, the nation's capital, the leaders of the Canadian government wanted to do something special to celebrate. But it was not going to be easy. The Members of Parliament, who represented many different political parties in the House of Commons, were more accustomed to opposing each other than working together.

Commemorative stamp: *O Canada* music
Copyright Canada Post Corporations, 1980.
Reproduced with Permission

But for once, they chose to agree. On June 27th, 1980, the Honourable Francis Fox, Canada's Secretary of State, stood up in the House of Commons. Since World War I, he began, everyone, from soldiers to sailors to hockey players, has sung *O Canada*. To celebrate the renewed unity of Canada, Fox suggested the government should "set the example by enshrining one of the most unifying realities of our young collective history, *O Canada*."

A Gift to the Nation

IN 1980, THE 100TH BIRTHDAY of *O Canada*, the nation witnessed one of the worst crises in its history. The people of Québec voted on a plan to make their province a separate country. Luckily for Canada, the plan was rejected. About 60% of the voters in Québec chose to keep their province part of the country.

Canada remained united! In Ottawa, the nation's capital, the leaders of the Canadian government wanted to do something special to celebrate. But it was not going to be easy. The Members of Parliament, who represented many different political parties in the House of Commons, were more accustomed to opposing each other than working together.

But for once, they chose to agree. On June 27th, 1980, the Honourable Francis Fox, Canada's Secretary of State, stood up in the House of Commons. Since World War I, he began, everyone, from soldiers to sailors to hockey players, has sung *O Canada*. To celebrate the renewed unity of Canada, Fox suggested the government should "set the example by enshrining one of the most unifying realities of our young collective history, *O Canada*."

Commemorative stamp: *O Canada* music
Copyright Canada Post Corporations, 1980.
Reproduced with Permission

TIMELINE: 1940-1960

1942 — Japanese Canadians are forced into internment camps for the length of WWII, though no charges are ever laid.

1944 — Canadian troops land in Normandy on D-Day and take part in the liberation of Holland.

1945 — Maurice "Rocket" Richard of the Montreal Canadiens scores 50 goals in 50 games.

1947 — Canadian citizenship is introduced. Citizenship certificates help to shape a unique and independent Canadian identity.

1949 — Newfoundland joins Confederation, becoming Canada's 10th province.

1951 — The National Ballet of Canada is founded.

1952 — Canada's first television stations begin broadcasting from Toronto and Montreal.

1957 — Future Canadian Prime Minister Lester B. Pearson wins a Nobel Peace Prize for his work with the UN.

1960 — Canada's First Nations population wins the right to vote in federal elections.

1960 — The Canadian Bill of Rights is passed.

O   Ca - na   - da!   We   stand   on   guard   for   thee.
Pro - té - ge - ra   nos   foy - ers   et   nos   droits.

O   Ca - na   - da!   We   stand   on   guard   for   thee.
Pro - té - ge - ra   nos   foy - ers   et   nos   droits.

Mr. Fox wanted to change eight words in the English song, adding the phrases, "From far and wide" and "God keep our land." These suggested changes came from a committee that read over 1,000 letters written by Canadians about the national anthem. Not all the politicians in Ottawa agreed with the changes, but on that day, their differences were put aside. Each Member of Parliament voted in favour of the *National Anthem Act*. Then, at one o'clock, the entire House of Commons stood together and sang the new and official version of *O Canada*.

Five days later, on Canada's 113th birthday (then known as Dominion Day), 100,000 people gathered on Parliament Hill. At noon, under a scorching sun, Governor General Edward Schreyer, the Queen's representative, signed the royal proclamation, making *O Canada* official. Pierre Trudeau, then Prime Minister, announced to the crowd that the national anthem was the best present the country could have on its birthday. "Let us sing together this anthem to this country we truly love," said Trudeau, and the crowd burst into song. Lavallée's tune, composed so many years ago, had come a long way.

TIMELINE: 1960-1980

1962 The Trans-Canada Highway opens.

1965 Canada officially adopts the maple leaf flag.

1969 English and French are both recognized as official languages in Canada by the federal government.

1970 Ottawa invokes the War Measures Act in response to the Québec Crisis.

1972 Team Canada wins the Summit Hockey Series, beating out Team Soviet Union 6-5.

1975 Toronto's CN Tower is completed. It becomes the world's tallest free-standing structure.

1976 The Montreal Olympics begin. It is the first and only time to date that Canada has hosted the Summer Olympics.

1980 Terry Fox's Marathon of Hope begins in St. John's, Newfoundland.

1980 Jeanne Sauvé is the first Canadian woman to be appointed Speaker of the House.

1980 100 years after its composition, *O Canada* is officially adopted as Canada's national anthem.